Guidance and Mark Schem
Reading: Levels 3–5

D0530097

Contents	Page

About this pack

This pack provides you with practice papers to help support children with the Levels 3–5 Reading test and to assess which skills need further development. The pack consists of this introductory booklet (including mark schemes) and three sample papers covering a wide range of Levels 3–5 content taken from the Key Stage 2 programme of study. A Reading Booklet and Answer Booklet is provided for each paper.

Deciding on children's suitability

To take the Levels 3–5 test, children should be working at Level 3 or above from early in their final year of Key Stage 2.

Below are the National Curriculum Attainment Targets for Levels 3, 4 and 5 for Reading.

Looking at these carefully, you can see the progression of skills and understanding through the levels.

Level 3

Pupils read a range of texts fluently and accurately. They read independently, using strategies appropriately to establish meaning. In responding to fiction and non-fiction they show understanding of the main points and express preferences. They use their knowledge of the alphabet to locate books and find information.

Level 4

In responding to a range of texts, pupils show understanding of significant ideas, themes, events and characters, beginning to use inference and deduction. They refer to the text when explaining their views. They locate and use ideas and information.

Level 5

Pupils show understanding of a range of texts, selecting essential points and using inference and deduction where appropriate. In their responses, they identify key features, themes and characters and select sentences, phrases and relevant information to support their views. They retrieve and collate information from a range of sources.

Assessment focuses for reading

The Reading paper uses Assessment Focuses (AFs) to categorise questions. For each of these areas a good degree of competence in demonstrating and explaining understanding is needed.

The seven AFs represent a development of reader cognition and as such AF1 is not explicitly tested in the papers.

Children are assessed on their ability to:

AF1 Use a range of strategies, including accurate decoding of text, to read for meaning.
(Not assessed by these tests.)

AF2 Understand, describe, select or retrieve information, events or ideas from texts and use quotation and reference to text.

AF3 Deduce, infer or interpret information, events or ideas from texts.

AF4 Identify and comment on the structure and organisation of texts, including grammatical and presentational features at text level.

AF5 Explain and comment on writers' use of language, including grammatical and literary features at word and sentence level.

AF6 Identify and comment on writers' purposes and viewpoints, and the overall effect of the text on the reader.

AF7 Relate texts to their social, cultural and historical contexts and literary traditions.

A grid showing the coverage of AFs, and the marks available for each question, is included at the end of the Answer booklet for each paper.

About the tests

Each reading test consists of three texts of different genres and contains 50 marks. Each test lasts for 1 hour.

- Reading Booklet: children may underline, highlight or make notes in the Reading Booklet.
- Answer Booklet: children may and should refer back to the Reading Booklet for their answers.

The range of marks available for each question is shown in the Answer Booklet next to each question and is also shown next to each answer in the teachers' mark scheme. Incorrect answers do not get a mark and no half marks should be given.

There are different types of answer:

- **Short answers:** Children will be asked to write a simple word or phrase and 1 mark may be given for a correct response.
- **Several line answers:** Children will need to write a phrase or a few sentences and up to 2 marks may be given.
- **Longer answers:** Children may be asked to give a more detailed explanation of their own opinion or of the author's intentions and up to 3 marks may be given.
- **Other answers:** Children may be required to match, tick or draw a ring around a correct answer.

Using the practice papers

The practice papers in this pack can be used as you would any other practice materials. The children will need to be familiar with specific test-focused skills, such as reading carefully, leaving questions if they seem too difficult, working at a suitable pace, and of course checking through their work.

If you choose to use the papers for looking at content rather than practising tests, do be aware of the time factor. The tests require a lot of work to be done in 1 hour as they are testing the degree of competence children have – it is not enough to be able to answer questions correctly but slowly.

Marking and assessing the papers

The mark schemes and answers are located in this booklet.

Marking is tricky: answers in literacy will be varied and subjective from child to child, and a fair degree of marker discretion and interpretation is needed, particularly if children's understanding and skills have to be deduced from their answers. The mark schemes provide detailed examples of correct answers (although other variations/phrasings are often acceptable) and an explanation about what the answer should contain to be awarded a mark or marks.

Although the mark scheme contains several suggestions for correct answers, for many questions, some children may find other ways of expressing a correct answer. When marking these tests, judgement needs to be exercised when assessing the accuracy or relevance of an answer and credit should be given for correct responses.

The thresholds for Levels 3, 4 and 5 vary each year according to difficulty levels. For the sample tests in this pack, the level thresholds below should be treated as a guideline. All tests have a maximum of 50 marks available.

Marks achieved	Level
0–10	Below Level 3
11–17	Level 3
18–32	Level 4
33–50	Level 5

Advice for parents

How this pack will help

This pack will support your child to get ready for the KS2 National Reading Tests commonly called SATs. It provides valuable practice and help at levels and content expected of Year 6 children aged 10–11 years.

In the weeks and sometimes months leading up to the National Tests, your child will be given plenty of practice, revision and tips to give them the best possible chance to demonstrate their knowledge and understanding. It is important to try to practise outside of school, and many children benefit from extra input, so this book will help your child prepare further and help to build their confidence and their ability to work to a time limit. Practice is vital, so every opportunity helps, but don't start too late.

In this book you will find three Reading tests. The layout and format of each test closely matches those used in the National Tests, so your child will become familiar with what to expect and get used to the style of the tests. In this booklet you will find a comprehensive answer section with notes and tips for children and guidance about how to mark the questions.

Tips

- Make sure that you allow your child to take the test in a quiet environment where they are not likely to be interrupted or distracted.
- Make sure your child has a flat surface to work on with plenty of space to spread out and good light.
- Emphasise the importance of reading and re-reading a question and to underline or circle any important information.
- These papers are similar to the one your child will take in May at the end of Year 6 and they therefore give you a good idea of strengths and areas for development. So, when you have found areas that require some more practice, it is useful to go over these again and practise similar types of questions with your child.
- Go through the tests again together, identify any gaps in learning and address any misconceptions or areas of misunderstanding. If you are unsure of anything yourself, then make an appointment to see your child's teacher who will be able to help and advise further.

Advice for children

What to do before the test

- Revise and practise on a regular basis.
- Spend at least 2 hours a week practising.
- Focus on the areas you are least confident in to get better.
- Get a good night's sleep and eat a wholesome breakfast.
- Be on time for school.
- Have all the necessary materials.
- Avoid stressful situations prior to a test.

SCHOLASTIC Guidance and Mark Schemes

Paper 1: Assessment Focus coverage, showing available marks

Question	AF2 Understand, describe, select or retrieve information, events or ideas from texts and use quotation and reference to text.	AF3 Deduce, infer or interpret information, events or ideas from texts.	AF4 Identify and comment on the structure and organisation of texts.	AF5 Explain and comment on writers' uses of language, including grammatical and literary features at word and sentence level.	AF6 Identify and comment on writers' purposes and viewpoints, and the overall effect of the text on the reader.	AF7 Relate texts to their social, cultural and historical contexts and literary traditions.
Text 1: *How to look after a rabbit*						
1	1					
2	1					
3 a & b			1 + 1			
4		1				
5		2				
6				1		
7					2	
Text 2: *Reaching Treasure Island*						
8	1					
9	1					
10		1				
11	1					
12	1					
13	1					
14	1					
15	1					
16				1		
17		2				
18				2		
19		1				
20	1					
21				1		
22					2	
23						2
Text 3: *Childhood in Victorian Britain*						
24	1					
25	2					
26		2				
27		1				
28	2					
29			2			
30					1	
31					1	
All three texts						
32						2
33		2				
34						2
35		2				
Total	**15**	**14**	**4**	**5**	**6**	**6**

Mark Scheme for Paper 1

Q	Answers	Mark	AF
1	**Award 1 mark for:** *They are friendly and fun.*	1	AF2
2	**Award 1 mark** for all three answers correct. Have time to look after it. Buy a hutch. Buy a carrying case for it.	1	AF2
3	**a) Award 1 mark** for answers such as: *It makes it clearer* or *It makes information easy to find.* **b) Award 1 mark** only if both the following are chosen: subheadings numbered points	1 1	AF4 AF4
4	**Award 1 mark** for any appropriate inference. For example: *To stop it getting lonely.* *So it gets used to people.* *To stop it getting bored.*	1	AF3
5	**Award 2 marks** for all four answers correctly matched. **Award 1 mark** for two correctly matched. Clean your rabbit's hutch – To prevent disease and illness Give your rabbit some wood to chew on – To stop their teeth becoming too long Check the hutch is in good condition – To stop the rabbit injuring itself Take it to the vets for an injection – To prevent myxomatosis	Up to 2	AF3
6	**Award 1 mark** for answers that correctly identify one of the following phrases: *can be complex* *you'll soon become accustomed*	1	AF5
7	**Award 2 marks** for reasonable answers which use two pieces of information taken from the text. **Award 1 mark** for an answer which uses one reference to the text. For example: **Yes:** ● *They are friendly and fun.* ● *You can play with them.* ● *You'll have lots of fun together.* **No:** ● *They are expensive to keep.* ● *It can be complex looking after them.* ● *You need time to look after them.* ● *You have to clean out their hutch/change their straw.* ● *You have to take it to the vets.* ● *You have to find someone to look after it if you go on holiday.* **Yes and No:** ● *Combination of above.*	Up to 2	AF6

 SCHOLASTIC Guidance and Mark Schemes

Q	Answers	Mark	AF
8	ship.	I	AF2
9	sunny.	I	AF2
10	threatening.	I	AF3
11	a ship.	I	AF2
12	rough.	I	AF2
13	to tow the ship to a safe place.	I	AF2
14	complained about doing it.	I	AF2
15	next morning.	I	AF2
16	**Award I mark** if all three features are correctly chosen. An introduction A glossary Paragraphs	I	AF5
17	**Award 2 marks** for any reasonable inference which gives evidence from the text. For example: *He did not like the island as it says he 'hated the very thought of Treasure Island'.* *He didn't want to be there because it looked 'grey' and 'sad'.* *He had expected to be glad to arrive but he was disappointed instead: 'My heart sank into my boots'.* *He was afraid of what might happen: 'I hated the very thought of Treasure Island'.* *He did not like the look of the island and said it looked 'strange'.* *He felt frightened: 'My heart sank into my boots'.* **Award I mark** if only an emotion or an appropriate quote is given.	Up to 2	AF3
18	**Award 2 marks** for two answers that give both an interpretation and a quote, such as: *The author shows us the sea is rough by saying the ship 'was rolling in the ocean swell'.* *He describes how the sea is making the boat move suddenly: 'jumping like an injured animal'.* *He describes the movement of the boat to show us that the sea is rough.* *The author describes the noises the boat is making to tell us that the sea is moving it about: 'The rudder was banging to and fro', 'The whole ship was creaking, groaning'.* *Jim tells us that he is being thrown around in the boat, so the sea must be rough: 'I had to cling tight to the rope'.* *The main character is 'being rolled about like a bottle' which tells us the boat is moving from side to side on the sea.* *It says the sea is 'Foaming and thundering on the steep beach'.* **Award I mark** for only one complete answer or two quotes without interpretation are given.	Up to 2	AF5

Q	Answers	Mark	AF
19	**Award 1 mark** for any of the following quotes (or phrases from within them): *The men grumbled fiercely over their work.* *The very sight of the island seemed to have made them give up working.* *If the behaviour of the sailors had been alarming in the boat, it became truly threatening when they had come back on board the Hispaniola.* *They lay about the deck growling together as they talked.* *The slightest order was received with a black look and grudgingly and carelessly obeyed.* *Mutiny it was plain, hung over us like a thunder cloud.*	1	AF3
20	To find treasure.	1	AF2
21	it's an unhealthy place to go.	1	AF5
22	**Award 2 marks** for answers that recognise the effect of the first-person narrator such as: *To help us understand the character's point of view.* *To make events seem more real.* *To show us how the main character feels.* *We feel as if the events are happening to us.* *To make us feel that someone is telling us a story of what happened to them.*	2	AF6
23	**Award 1 mark** for each correct answer. Dangerous and exciting events Heroic characters	Up to 2	AF7
24	**Award 1 mark** for all three answers: poor diets poor sanitation lack of health care	1	AF2
25	**Award 2 marks** for answers that include two of the following: *Richer children were well fed.* *Poor children looked hungry and were thin.* *Richer children wore warm clothes.* *Poor children had tatty clothes.* *Richer children had shoes on their feet.* *Poor children would be lucky if they wore shoes.* **Award 1 mark** if only one difference is listed.	Up to 2	AF2
26	**Award 2 marks** for answers that select both: Rich parents could afford education. Poorer children did not need education for the jobs they would do. **Award 1 mark** for only one correct answer.	Up to 2	AF3
27	**Award 1 mark** for answers that correctly recognise the danger involved or that the government made school compulsory, such as: *Children were too young to work underground. The work was too hard and dangerous for them. Mines were dark, dangerous places.* *Children needed to be in school.*	1	AF3

Q	Answers	Mark	AF
28	**Award 2 marks** for any two appropriate differences such as: *No television.* *Children didn't have to go to school until 1880.* *No plastic – affected toys.* *Big divide between rich and poor.* *High death rate.* *Children worked in dangerous jobs.* *Children worked at early age.* **Award 1 mark** if only one difference is listed.	Up to 2	AF2
29	**Award 2 marks** for answers such as: *To encourage the reader to find out more.* *To try to get children to research about Victorian children.* *To show that there is more information to find. To talk to the reader and make them feel more involved.*	2	AF4
30	The author includes expert information.	1	AF6
31	To inform us about Victorian lives.	1	AF6
32	**Award 2 marks** for a fully correct answer.	Up to 2	AF7

	About any time	About the present	About the past
Childhood in Victorian Britain			✓
Reaching Treasure Island			✓
How to look after a rabbit	✓		

Award 1 mark for 2 correct answers.

Q	Answers	Mark	AF
33	**Award 2 marks** for a fully correct answer. It was a very frightening place. – Reaching Treasure Island Let the fun begin! – How to look after a rabbit Few of us would want to have lived then. – Childhood in Victorian Britain **Award 1 mark** for 2 correct answers.	Up to 2	AF3

Q	Answers	Mark	AF
34	**Award 2 marks** for a fully correct answer. **Text** **Pages** a factual account **7–8** a fictional adventure **5–6** an instructional text **3–4** **Award 1 mark** for 2 correct answers.	Up to 2	AF7
35	**Award 2 marks** for a fully correct answer.	Up to 2	AF3

Statement	True	False
Rabbits make great pets.	✓	
Green-coloured woods covered a large part of the surface of Treasure Island.		✓
If you were poor in Victorian Britain, you could expect to be working from the age of five or younger.	✓	
All children had to go to school in Victorian Britain from 1860 onwards.		✓

Award 1 mark for 3 correct answers.

The thresholds for Levels 3, 4 and 5 vary each year according to difficulty levels. For the sample tests in this pack, the level thresholds below should be treated as a guideline. All tests have a maximum of 50 marks available.

Marks achieved	Level
0–10	Below Level 3
11–17	Level 3
18–32	Level 4
33–50	Level 5

Paper 2: Assessment Focus coverage, showing available marks

Question	AF2 Understand, describe, select or retrieve information, events or ideas from texts and use quotation and reference to text.	AF3 Deduce, infer or interpret information, events or ideas from texts.	AF4 Identify and comment on the structure and organisation of texts.	AF5 Explain and comment on writers' uses of language.	AF6 Identify and comment on writers' purposes and viewpoints, and the overall effect of the text on the reader.	AF7 Relate texts to their social, cultural and historical contexts and literary traditions.
Text 1: *Cool uniform*						
1	2					
2					1	
3					1	
4			1			
5	1					
6	1					
7		1				
8			1			
9	1					
10					2	
Text 2: *A London Cab Horse*						
11	1					
12	1					
13		1				
14				1		
15		1				
16	1					
17		1				
18				1		
19				1		
20		1				
21						1
22		3				
23a & b					1 + 1	
24	2					
Text 3: *Modern-day piracy*						
25	1					
26		2				
27			1			
28a	1					
28b		1				
29	2					
30	1					
31	1					
32		2				
33					2	
All three texts						
34		2				
35			2			
36					2	
Total	16	15	5	3	10	1

Mark Scheme for Paper 2

Q	Answers	Mark	AF
1	**Award 2 marks** for all five correct answers. *dark trousers* *a white shirt* *the school tie* *a black blazer with the school badge on it* *a cap* **Award 1 mark** if three or more of the following are listed.	Up to 2	AF2
2	give the reader information about school uniforms.	1	AF6
3	understand why uniforms have not changed much.	1	AF6
4	not in order.	1	AF4
5	hats and caps.	1	AF2
6	**Award 1 mark** for either of the following quotes: *It's because they are what people blindly expect to wear to school.* *very few people have seen a need for it.*	1	AF2
7	**Award 1 mark** for answers that infer: *parents expect uniforms to be worn and so would be unhappy if they were not* or *the school's reputation could suffer.*	1	AF3
8	**Award 1 mark** for answers that recognise that the ellipsis suggests a negative implication such as: *The school will be seen to be scruffy.* *The school will be seen as unsuccessful.* *The school's reputation will be damaged.* *The writer thinks it is obvious that it would be bad for the school.*	1	AF4
9	**Award 1 mark** for both names Gok Wan and Stella McCartney **Award no marks** if only one name is given.	1	AF2
10	**Award 2 marks** for any two quotes that correctly suggest the author's negative view of current uniform or positive view of possible change, such as: He says 'the brave step of doing away with uniforms completely'. 'Why has there been no progress?' 'Why? Why? Why?' He asks why fashion has changed but uniforms have not. 'what people blindly expect their children to wear to school'. 'You go to school, you wear the uniform. End of story.' He thinks that modern designers would create 'Something smart, distinctive and trendy'. He calls a new uniform 'A cool uniform'. **Award 1 mark** if only one answer is given.	Up to 2	AF6
11	Jerry.	1	AF2

■SCHOLASTIC Guidance and Mark Schemes

Q	Answers	Mark	AF
12	fine mannered.	I	AF2
13	kind and gentle.	I	AF3
14	it was difficult.	I	AF5
15	he didn't whip his horses.	I	AF3
16	with plenty of room to turn around.	I	AF2
17	it would make them uncomfortable.	I	AF3
18	**Award I mark** only if both correct answers are chosen: It is autobiographical. The storyteller is an animal.	I	AF5
19	**Award I mark** for answers that refer to any one of the following quotes: *It was a great treat to be petted again and talked to in a gentle voice* *the broken knees* *the 'Black Beauty' of olden times*	I	AF5
20	**Award I mark** for any sensible reason, such as: *He likes people.* *He wanted to be well treated.* *He wanted more kindness/titbits.* *He is grateful for being treated nicely.*	I	AF3
21	**Award I mark** for answers that use information from the text. For example: *It says that Captain was in the Crimean War.* *Cabs are not pulled by horses now.* *There are carts and carriages on the streets in the story, but we have cars.*	I	AF7
22	**Award 3 marks** for six correct reasons. Advantages, any three of: *Jerry's family were kind.* *He wasn't whipped.* *They talked to him in a gentle voice.* *He liked working with Captain.* *He and his master understood each other well.* *They were kept clean, fed and watered.* *They had Sunday off.* Disadvantages, any three of: *It was very trying.* *London streets were noisy.* *It made him feel anxious and harassed (at first).* *He had to pull a cab.* *They worked so hard in the week.* **Award 2 marks** for four or more correct reasons. **Award I mark** for two or more correct reasons.	Up to 3	AF3

Q	Answers	Mark	AF
23	**a) Award 1 mark** for answers that recognise the effect of the viewpoint, such as: *So we can understand his feelings.* *So we can see it from his point of view.* *So we feel more involved.*	1	AF6
	b) animal welfare is important.	1	AF6
24	**Award 2 marks** for any answer which includes two of the following: *He was proud/old/tall/splendid/white.* *He went to the Crimean war as a young horse.* *He belonged to an officer in the cavalry.* *He used to lead the regiment.* *He is now a London cab horse.* **Award 1 mark** if only one of these is referred to.	Up to 2	AF2
25	**Award 1 mark** if all three answers are correctly chosen. have hearts of gold. are handsome. are attractive.	1	AF2
26	**Award 2 marks** for answers which include two pieces of information from the text, such as: *They are ruthless criminals.* *They are dangerous.* *They are not romantic.* *They aren't funny (don't tell jokes, don't talk Pirate).* *They don't wear pirate outfits (striped T-shirts, eye-patches or wooden legs).* *They use speed boats/rifles/rocket-propelled grenades.* *They attack all kinds of ships.* **Award 1 mark** if only one reference is made to the text.	Up to 2	AF3
27	**Award 1 mark** for answers such as: *It tells us he wishes they didn't exist now.* *He thinks they are a very bad thing.*	1	AF4
28	**a) Award 1 mark** for either: *Off the coast of Somalia* or *In Somalia*	1	AF2
	b) Award 1 mark for answers which infer reasons from the text such as: *Somalia is a poor country.* *The pirates used to be fishermen but cannot fish any longer.*	1	AF3
29	**Award 2 marks** for all answers correctly matched: Many pirates used to be – fishermen. Successful pirates have – big houses and flashy cars. Accountants manage the – money of some pirates. In poor countries piracy is seen as – an acceptable business activity. **Award 1 mark** if only two are correctly matched.	Up to 2	AF2
30	kidnapping crews and demanding ransoms	1	AF2

■■SCHOLASTIC Guidance and Mark Schemes

Q	Answers	Mark	AF
31	**Award 1 mark** for the correct answer: *International naval patrols are making it harder for pirates.*	1	AF2
32	**Award 2 marks** for two answers such as: *He thinks that Captain Philips shows a more realistic view of piracy.* *The writer says the film shows events from Captain Phillips' point of view, which is new.* *He believes the film shows how violent the pirates are for the first time.* *The writer thinks that Hollywood has now made the Captain the hero, not the pirates.* *Earlier films were a romantic/glamourised view of piracy and showed it from the pirate's, not the victims' viewpoint.* *Before, Hollywood made the pirates look handsome, good-hearted, heroic but this film shows the horror of an attack.* **Award 1 mark** if only one answer is given.	Up to 2	AF3
33	**Award 2 marks** for any relevant phrase with explanation, such as: *'It would be nice if the movie version of pirates was correct' tells us that the author thinks that the movies have been wrong to show pirates this way.* *'There is some good news' tells us he is pleased that pirate attacks are decreasing.* *'Tom Hanks, plays the ship's brave captain, Richard Phillips' suggests he admires the real captain and is on his side.* *'if it does not make a lot of money' suggests the author thinks Hollywood is only interested in making money and doesn't care about the message its films give.* **Award 1 mark** if only a phrase or an explanation is given.	Up to 2	AF6
34	**Award 2 marks** for all correct answers. <table><tr><th>Statement</th><th>True</th><th>False</th></tr><tr><td>Captain was a small, white, rather small-boned animal.</td><td></td><td>✓</td></tr><tr><td>Black Beauty went out with the cab every afternoon.</td><td>✓</td><td></td></tr><tr><td>School uniforms have changed little since the 1950s.</td><td>✓</td><td></td></tr><tr><td>Modern-day pirates have striped T-shirts, eye patches and wooden legs.</td><td></td><td>✓</td></tr></table> **Award 1 mark** for three correct answers.	Up to 2	AF3
35	**Award 2 marks** for answers with a reference to *Black Beauty* to demonstrate the differences. For example: *The subheadings tell the reader what each section is about. Black Beauty is continuous text with nothing to break the text up. This makes it harder to follow.* **Award 1 mark** for any reason.	Up to 2	AF4

Q	Answers	Mark	AF
36	**Award 2 marks** for two points made with appropriate examples. For example: *Allows the author to show more than one viewpoint.* *Allows the author to be neutral or to be biased.* *Allows the writer to seem to know everything.* *Allows the writer to ask questions and then answer them.* Cool uniform examples: *What about the girls? It's almost the same! With very few variations, the uniforms that pupils will wear to go to their secondary schools will be almost identical to those of their grandparents!* *Why would this be a brave move? Well, it seems that the main reason schools have uniforms is that parents expect them.* *Could they come up with something completely different that would please pupils and parents alike? Something smart, distinctive and trendy. A cool uniform.* Modern-day pirates examples: *The rewards of piracy are tempting.* *There is some good news.* *However, if the film does not make a lot of money, you can be sure that the big film companies will go back to glamorising the pirates.* **Award 1 mark** if only an explanation is given with one quote.	Up to 2	AF6

The thresholds for Levels 3, 4 and 5 vary each year according to difficulty levels. For the sample tests in this pack, the level thresholds below should be treated as a guideline. All tests have a maximum of 50 marks available.

Marks achieved	Level
0–10	Below Level 3
11–17	Level 3
18–32	Level 4
33–50	Level 5

Paper 3: Assessment Focus coverage, showing available marks

Question	AF2 Understand, describe, select or retrieve information, events or ideas from texts and use quotation and reference to text.	AF3 Deduce, infer or interpret information, events or ideas from texts.	AF4 Identify and comment on the structure and organisation of texts, including grammatical and presentational features at text level.	AF5 Explain and comment on writers' uses of language, including grammatical and literary features at word and sentence level.	AF6 Identify and comment on writers' purposes and viewpoints, and the overall effect of the text on the reader.	AF7 Relate texts to their social, cultural and historical contexts and literary traditions.
Text 1: *Hannah's helping hand*						
1	1					
2	1					
3			2			
4				1		
5	2					
6		2				
Text 2: *Courageous animals*						
7	2					
8				2		
9		1				
10	1					
11	1					
12	1					
13		1				
14	2					
15					2	
16			2			
17					2	
Text 3: *Into the Underworld*						
18	2					
19		2				
20		2				
21		1				
22		1				
23	1					
24		2				
25				1		
26	1					
27					2	
28				2		
29		1				
All three texts						
30		2				
31					3	
32					1	
Total	15	15	4	6	10	0

Mark Scheme for Paper 3

Q	Answers	Mark	AF
1	*To solve your problems.*	1	AF2
2	**Award 1 mark** for both answers correct: It is cheap. It is quick to make. **Award no marks** if only one correct answer is chosen.	1	AF2
3	**Award 2 marks** for all answers correctly matched as follows: Text boxes – Divide the information into separate parts Links (<u>Pirate</u> and <u>Next</u>) – So that the reader can click to find more information Numbered steps – Make it easy to follow the order Words in italics – Help to show which words are spoken Pictures – Show examples of costumes **Award 1 mark** if three are correctly matched.	Up to 2	AF4
4	**Award 1 mark** for answers that recognise: *that she uses* you *or* your *so that we feel we are being spoken to.* *the use of questions such as* What are you going to wear? *which make us feel more involved.* *the friendly and informal style (exclamations, incomplete sentences:* Gorilla? Space traveller?*).* *that she tells us what to do with instructions such as* Remember, don't despair.	1	AF5
5	**Award 2 marks** where all answers are correct.	Up to 2	AF2

Statement	True	False
You need lots of designer labels on your outfit.		✓
You can paint your top with horizontal lines.	✓	
Cut the legs off the jeans in a jagged pattern.	✓	
Make a metal sword and telescope.		✓
Draw a large earring on a piece of card.		✓

Award 1 mark if three or more are correct.

■SCHOLASTIC Guidance and Mark Schemes

Q	Answers	Mark	AF
6	**Award 2 marks** for an opinion with any reference to the text. For example: Yes: *It gives clear instructions on how to make the outfit.* *It tells you how to make a hat, eye-patch, sword and telescope, which are all things pirates would have.* *It tells you how to finish off your outfit with an earring which is a really good idea.* *It suggests some pirate talk to make it more realistic.* No: *Home made things never look good.* *There are too many steps and it sounds hard work.* *I didn't understand how to make... (the sword/telescope).* *I would have liked templates/diagrams to show me what the hat/sword/ telescope should look like.* **Award no marks** if only 'Yes' or 'No' is given.	Up to 2	AF3
7	**Award 2 marks** for any two of the following: *Cares for the pets of people in need/provides free veterinary care* *Encourages responsible pet ownership* *Recognises the achievements of animals/ gives awards for bravery* **Award 1 mark** if only one is listed.	Up to 2	AF2
8	**Award 2 marks** if all four are correctly matched: gallantry – bravery devotion – dedication/loyalty exploits – feats/achievements atrocious – dreadful **Award 1 mark** if only two are matched correctly.	2	AF5
9	**Award 1 mark** for answers that recognise that pigeons carried messages in dangerous situations. For example: *Because they were used to carry messages over dangerous land.* *They risked getting shot at/injured while carrying messages.*	1	AF3
10	Because they led their blind owners to safety after the 9/11 attack	1	AF2
11	**Award 1 mark** for answers that include reference to Brian becoming a paratrooper.	1	AF2
12	The Dickin Medal	1	AF2
13	**Award 1 mark** for answers that include a logical reason inferred from the text, such as: *The Dickin Medal has been awarded since 1943, but the Gold Medal only started in 2002.* *Animals have to show great bravery to get the award.* *Animals in the armed forces have more opportunities to show bravery and devotion.*	1	AF3

Q	Answers	Mark	AF
14	**Award 2 marks** for answers that refer to both of the following: *He found lost students in atrocious weather.* *He saved two people trapped in rubble after an earthquake in Turkey.* **Award 1 mark** for only one correct answer.	Up to 2	AF2
15	**Award 2 marks** for answers which both list a word or phrase and explain how it shows the author's attitude. For example: *'quite remarkable' – shows he is full of admiration towards them* *'remained loyally' – shows he likes their devotion* *'amazingly'– shows that the author sees this as very unusual and fantastic* *'no less amazing'– suggests that the author thinks they deserve their medals as much as those who got the Dickin Medal* Accept any other appropriate references, with explanations. **Award 1 mark** where only an appropriate word or phrase is listed, with no explanation.	Up to 2	AF6
16	**Award 2 marks** where all four features are correctly matched to their purposes. Title – To tell us what the whole passage is about Photographs – To show us something in the passage Italics – To make words or phrases stand out Text boxes – To break information into smaller chunks **Award 1 mark** for two correct matches.	Up to 2	AF4
17	**Award 2 marks** for any two references to that animal's achievement. Accept the name of any animal in the text. For example: *Lulu, the kangaroo who saved a farmer injured by a falling tree. I liked the way she got the attention of his family so he could be rescued. It impressed me because it is a wild animal but still knew the farmer needed help.* **Award 1 mark** if only one reason is given. **Award no marks** for the name of the animal.	Up to 2	AF6
18	**Award 2 marks** for all answers numbered correctly, as follows: The voice in the trunk — 5 James climbing the bell tower — 1 James putting on the cloak — 3 James opening the trunk — 2 James' father opening the trunk — 6 James' father calling to James — 4 **Award 1 mark** for 3 or more answers in the correct order.	Up to 2	AF2

■SCHOLASTIC Guidance and Mark Schemes

Q	Answers	Mark	AF
19	**Award 2 marks** for any answers that infer two of the following ideas: *He was worried that his father would be missing him.* *He was sad to have to leave.* *He was concerned that he needed to get down quickly.* *He wanted to get down before he got into trouble.* **Award 1 mark** if only one idea is included.	Up to 2	AF3
20	**Award 2 marks** for any two of the following: *'He dare not be caught up there.'* *'Punishment, if not an eye for an eye, a tooth for a tooth, would at least require him to turn the other cheek.'* *'In panic'* *'whatever his father would do to him.'* **Award 1 mark** if only one phrase or sentence is included.	Up to 2	AF3
21	**Award 1 mark** for any one of the following: *His father.* *The church service.* *The boredom of Sundays.*	1	AF3
22	**Award 1 mark** for any answer that suggests one of the following: *It was too high.* *It was dangerous.* *There was nothing in the bell tower.* *He had no need to go there.*	1	AF3
23	**Award 1 mark** for: *a ventriloquist's dummy.*	1	AF2
24	**Award 2 marks** if both of the following phrases are selected: What a let-down there seemed little of interest **Award 1 mark** if only one is chosen.	Up to 2	AF3
25	**Award 1 mark** for answers which recognise why the feature is used, such as: *It makes you wonder what could happen and want to know the answer.* *It builds tension.* *It makes the reader feel how much James wants to know what is in the chest.*	1	AF5
26	**Award 1 mark** for one of the following answers: *The dust* or *A storm of dust.*	1	AF2

Q	Answers	Mark	AF
27	**Award 2 marks** for answers which both describe the ending and recognise its effect, such as: *It is an open ending which makes us want to continue reading.* *It makes it more exciting because we do not know what has happened to James and start to imagine where he might be.* *It is shocking to the reader because they were expecting James to be in trouble but he is gone, so they want to find out where he is.* **Award 1 mark** for answers which only describe the ending, or the effect, such as: *It is a 'cliffhanger' ending.* *It is a surprise.* *It makes the ending exciting.*	Up to 2	AF6
28	**Award 2 marks** for answers that identify two tense moments in the story such as: *James being surprised by his father's voice at the bottom of the stairs.* *James' father coming up the stairs.* *When James first hears the voice from the trunk.* *James' father seeing the trunk.* *The trunk being empty when James' father opens it.* **Award 1 mark** if only one tense moment is listed.	Up to 2	AF5
29	**Award 1 mark** for reasonable inferences such as: *There isn't an alternative.* *To hide from his father.* *Because the voice tells him to.* *Because he panics.*	1	AF3
30	**Award 2 marks** for all answers correct. 	**Hannah's helping hand**	The website helps people to create pirate costumes/solve their problems.
Into the Underworld	The voice in the box helps James hide from his father.
Courageous animals	The animals help people in danger. | **Award 1 mark** for two answers correct.	Up to 2	AF3

■SCHOLASTIC Guidance and Mark Schemes

Q	Answers	Mark	AF
31	**Award 3 marks** for explaining the difference in language and giving an example from *Into the Underworld* and another text. For example: *Into the Underworld is an imaginative story/fiction/fantasy.* *It uses descriptive language and dialogue. It allows us to understand James' thoughts and feelings.* Examples: *A river of rain ran down the stained glass window.* *The great bell tower loomed above James like a signpost to the heavens.* *Today would be different. Today he would escape!* *What a let-down!* *With some regret, James closed the lid of the trunk and turned towards the staircase.* *"Oh my God!"* *James looked around helplessly for a place to hide. He dare not be caught up there* *Hannah's helping hand aims to inform and use impersonal, formal language. It feels like the writer is speaking directly to the reader.* Examples: *Yippee!!! You've been invited to a party!* *Oh dear, you have to go in fancy dress.* *If the answer to these questions is "No", don't despair. Go as a pirate.* *Learn some Pirate Talk – Shiver me timbers, me hearties, yer ready to walk the plank!* *Courageous animals aims to inform and uses formal language. It makes the author sound like an expert on the subject.* Examples: *The medal is made of bronze and has "For Gallantry" and "We also serve" inside a laurel wreath engraved upon it.* *Between 1943 and 1949 it was awarded 54 times, mostly to message-carrying pigeons* *In Australia, a kangaroo called Lulu received the RSPCA Purple Cross for saving the life of a farmer by alerting his family after he was knocked unconscious by a falling tree in a storm.*	Up to 3	AF6
32	**Award 1 mark** for all three correct.	1	AF6

Text	Fictional	Persuasive	Informative
Hannah's helping hand			✓
Into the Underworld	✓		
Courageous Animals			✓

The thresholds for Levels 3, 4 and 5 vary each year according to difficulty levels. For the sample tests in this pack, the level thresholds below should be treated as a guideline. All tests have a maximum of 50 marks available.

Marks achieved	Level
0–10	Below Level 3
11–17	Level 3
18–32	Level 4
33–50	Level 5

Notes

Notes

Notes

SCHOLASTIC

Practice Papers for the National Tests

Paper 1

Reading booklet   **Test paper**

Reading Levels 3-5

100% in line with the National Tests!

✓ **Prepare with confidence for the National Tests (SATs)**
These tests are the most authentic practice papers available for the Levels 3–5 Reading Test

✓ **All the support you need!**
Each test comes with a full mark scheme and clear guidance so you can check progress

✓ **Great value for money!**
In this pack you get three complete tests, including full-colour reading booklets, detailed answers, additional support and guidance

Paper 2

Reading booklet   **Test paper**

Paper 3

Reading booklet   **Test paper**

Guidance and Mark Schemes

Look out for the other great 'Practice Papers'

Grammar, Punctuation and Spelling Levels 3–5
ISBN 978-1407-12810-8

Maths Levels 3–5
ISBN 978-1407-12848-1

Reading Level 6
ISBN 978-1407-12812-2

Practice Papers for
Reading Levels 3–5

£7.99

SCHOLASTIC

ISBN 978-1-407-12847-4

9 781407 128474

A-125-808